E. W. Metcalf

Scientific research on alcoholics as medicine

E. W. Metcalf

Scientific research on alcoholics as medicine

ISBN/EAN: 9783337717773

Printed in Europe, USA, Canada, Australia, Japan

Cover: Foto ©ninafisch / pixelio.de

More available books at **www.hansebooks.com**

ALCOHOLIC ███ MEDICINE

COMPIL███

"I do not know of any que███ ████ more deeply than on this question o███

"Never in our course as a p███ ████ with the public in a more serious or ████ ████ cu-ARDSON.

"If a serious error has been ████ ████, let us correct the error as soon as prac████ ████ may." —Dr. JOHN BLACKMER.

"We ought not to rest sa████ ████ror, but we ought also to make every ████ ████ upheld one of the most fatal delusions ████ ████ind."— Dr. CHEYNE of Dublin.

THOMAS M████ ● ██████ █████ington, D. C.

By N. S. DAVIS, M.D., LL.D.,

PROFESSOR OF PRACTICAL AND CLINICAL MEDICINE IN THE
CHICAGO MEDICAL COLLEGE, MEDICAL DEPART-
MENT OF NORTHWESTERN UNIVERSITY.

By alcoholic liquors in the following paper is meant all
the varieties of fermented and distilled preparations con-
taining alcohol, such as beer, ale, porter, wine, whisky,
brandy, rum, gin, etc.; and my principal object is to give
an intelligible answer to the often-repeated inquiry whether
any one or all of these articles are really necessary for use
in the practice of medicine where the paramount objects
are to prevent, to palliate, or to cure disease in the safest
and most expeditious manner. To do this properly three
preliminary questions must be considered and, if possible,
settled on a basis of well-ascertained facts :

1. Do any of these liquids contain ingredients of value
to the sick, besides the alcohol they contain, that cannot be
furnished just as well from other sources ?

2. What are the appreciable effects of alcohol on the
human system both in health and disease ?

3. What are the conditions in sickness that it is calculated to remove ?

Every one who has given careful attention to the subject
will promptly answer the first question in the negative.

That the different varieties of beer and other fermented
drinks contain a small amount of fæcula or modified starch,
sugar, and a little saline matter capable of being appropri-
ated as nourishment, is true; but the quantity is so small
that it is practically useless.

The careful and repeated analyses of different varieties
of beer made by Liebig, Playfair, Hassels, and others show

that it would require the drinking of more than six barrels of beer to get enough of the nutritive materials just named to make the equivalent of one ordinary loaf of bread. Hence no well-informed person would think of using those drinks to obtain fæcula, sugar, or saline matters when the same materials could be obtained so much more readily and cheaply from other sources. The same remark is equally applicable to the active principle of hops in beer and that of juniper in gin. An infusion or tea prepared from one pennyworth of either would exert more influence than could be obtained from the same ingredients as they exist in a gallon of beer or a quart of gin. We may repeat, therefore, with emphasis, that there are no elements in any of the fermented and distilled liquors in sufficient quantity to be of the slightest value, either as nourishment or medicine, except the alcohol and water. So true is this that one would search the world over in vain to find any one using a specimen of fermented or distilled liquid after the alcohol generated by the fermentation had been separated from it.

Assuming it to be a fact that it is the alcohol in all these liquids, and that alone, which is capable of exerting any important influence upon the human system, I shall proceed to answer the second question, namely, What are the appreciable effects of alcohol on the human system both in health and disease? Having made this question one of special study and observation for more than forty years, I could easily fill a moderate-sized volume with the details of experiments, clinical observations and facts bearing upon the subject, and affording an ample basis for the conclusions I shall briefly state in this paper. I well remember when, in accordance with the simple and fascinating chemico-physiological doctrines of Liebig and his school, alcoholic liquors were classed with the hydro-carbons as "respiratory food," and almost universally regarded as capable of increasing the temperature of the human body and of stimulating all its functions. But when the investigations of Drs. Prout, of London, Sandras and Bouchardet, of France, and Böker, of Germany, confirmed by many others, had fully established the fact that during the presence of alcohol in the system the elimination of carbonic-acid gas from the lungs was diminished, together with a general diminution of waste matter from all the excretory organs, the idea of combustion or "respiratory food" had to be abandoned. This abandonment of the stimulating and heat-producing qualities of alcoholic drinks was rendered more complete when, in 1850, the writer of this paper proved by a carefully-executed series of experiments, in which the direct application of the thermometer was made to the subject operated on, that the presence of alcohol actually reduced the temperature of the body, and lessened the action of all the smaller blood vessels by lessening the sensibility of the vaso-motor nerves.

These results have since been fully established by the experimental investigations of Drs. B. W. Richardson and Anstie, of England, and Dr. Hammond, myself, and others in this country.

But no sooner had the most carefully-conducted scientific investigations proved the entire fallacy of the doctrine that alcohol was capable of stimulating or increasing the functions and temperature of the human body, than the advocates of its use reversed the grounds on which such advocacy was based. Accepting the well-established fact that the presence of alcohol in the system directly diminishes both the molecular changes and nerve sensibility, thereby retarding tissue changes, they claim that such retardation of molecular changes and excretory eliminations, by retarding the *waste*, was equivalent to the same amount of supply, and consequently that alcoholic drinks were "indirect food." As stated by Dr. Hammond, if the presence of alcohol, taken in the form of alcoholic drinks, lessened the sum-total of eliminations from the human body to the extent of half a pound in twenty-four hours, it was equivalent in value to half a pound of food taken. This idea, thus originating with men of known scientific reputation, rapidly became popular, and again furnished all classes with a plausible reason for taking whatever alcoholic beverage their fancy or tastes might dictate. But a critical examination will show that this position rests on no better foundation than the preceding one of combustion and increased heat. That the presence of alcohol in the system actually retards molecular changes, and consequently diminishes the aggregate amount of waste in a given time, is a well-established fact; but the inference drawn from this, that such diminution of *waste* is equivalent to the addition of an equal amount of new matter through the processes of digestion and assimilation, is entirely fallacious.

Those who have drawn this inference have apparently forgotten two of the most important physiological laws relating to animal life—namely, first, that all the active phenomena of life depend upon and directly involve molecular changes, and consequently necessitate both waste and supply; second, that every cell or organized atom of living animal matter has only a limited duration of integrity or life, at the end of which it must either undergo a natural disintegration into waste matter, or degenerate into an unhealthy and lower type of organization. Therefore, whatever retards the natural molecular changes in living tissues retards or lessens the phenomena of life, as seen in the diminution of secretion, excretion, temperature, and nerve sensibility; and by retaining cells and organized atoms beyond the natural limit of time directly promotes their degeneration into materials of a useless or positively injurious character, as when nervous, muscular, or secretory structure changes into atheromatous, fatty, caseous, or septic materials, instead of undergoing natural dissolution and excretion as waste matter. Hence, the prevention of a certain amount of waste of living structure in a given time is in no proper sense physiologically equivalent to the addition of an equal amount of new material by nutrition in the same time. On the contrary, both experiments and common observations show that whenever such mental or physical exercise is continued as naturally increases tissue changes and waste, and these are retarded or prevented by the presence of some agent capable of exerting such an influence, derangements of structure or function invariably follow. Assuming the foregoing statements to be correct, it is not difficult to understand the important effects of alcohol upon the structures and functions of the human body. Taken into the stomach diluted with water, as in all the varieties of the fermented and distilled drinks, it is rapidly absorbed, and enters into the blood unchanged, and circulates with it through all the organized structures of the body. This has been proved by a large number of analytical examinations, and the proof may be repeated at any time by applying the proper tests to the blood or tissues in from one to three hours after the alcoholic drink has been swallowed. While it is thus present in the blood, circulating in contact with all the tissues of the body, its strong affinity for the albuminous constituents they contain causes it to hold the natural molecular changes in check, and thereby retard the formation of the products of those changes, as seen in the diminution of temperature and the quantity of eliminations. It is not the eliminations alone that are diminished by this interference with the natural affinities of the blood, but the taking up of the oxygen from the air-cells of the lungs is retarded in equal ratio with the lessening of the amount of waste carbonic-acid gas liberated, thereby diminishing the necessary change from venous to arterial blood.

When the amount of the alcohol taken is small, but regularly repeated, as in the daily use of beer and wine, the diminished supply of oxygen to the tissues, coupled with the moderate retardation of waste, encourages the accumulation of unoxydated materials in the form of inert fat. This causes increased weight and bulk with corresponding decrease of activity and power of endurance, and if continued until past the middle period of life ends in fatty degenerations in the coats of the vessels of the brain, in the heart, the liver, or the kidneys, by which the natural duration of life is shortened by ten or fifteen years. When the quantity taken is greater and more concentrated, as in the free use of whisky, brandy, etc , not only are the molecular changes more actively retarded, leading to more rapid tissue degenerations, but the functions of the stomach and brain are so actively interfered with as to prevent healthy nutrition, and often induce either chronic inflammations or delirium tremens, or both.

Another important effect of alcohol while present in the blood is the direct diminution of sensibility in the brain and nervous structures of the body. It is this anæsthetic effect upon the cerebral and nervous structures that induces all the series of changes in the individual from simple don't-care-ativeness and unrestrained hilarity to stupor or dead-drunkenness, which chiefly occupies the attention of the public. It is in no sense a stimulant or tonic, either at the beginning, middle, or end of its effects, as it is generally supposed, but exerts a direct sedative effect upon nerve sensibility, by which the mind becomes less conscious of outward impressions of any kind, whether of heat, cold, weariness, weakness or pain, and in like ratio less capable of exercising self-control, or manifesting the usual sense of propriety.

It is this anæsthetic effect of alcohol that has led to all the popular errors and contradictory uses which have proved so destructive to human health and happiness. It has long been one of the noted paradoxes of human action that the same individual would resort to the same alcoholic drink to warm him in winter, protect him from the heat in summer, to strengthen when weak or weary, and to soothe

7

and cheer when afflicted in body or mind. With the facts now before us, the explanation of all this is apparent. The alcohol does not relieve the individual from cold by increasing his temperature; nor from heat by cooling him; nor from weakness and exhaustion by nourishing his tissues; nor yet from affliction by increasing nerve power, but simply by diminishing the sensibility of his nerve structures, and thereby lessening his consciousness of impressions, whether from cold or heat, or weariness or pain. In other words, the presence of the alcohol has not in any degree lessened the effects of the evils to which he is exposed, but has diminished his consciousness of their existence, and thereby impaired his judgment concerning the degree of their action upon him.

It is this property of alcohol to produce that sense of ease, buoyancy, and exhilaration arising from a moderate diminution of nerve sensibility that gives it the fascinating and delusive power over the human race which it has wielded for centuries gone by.

Finally, the alcohol, having entered the blood from the stomach unchanged, is incapable of assimilation or appropriation to the tissues of the body as nutritive material, and is separated from the blood and eliminated as foreign matter through the lungs, skin, kidneys, and other excretory organs, as fully proved by the experiments of Lallemand, Perrin, and Duroy, Richardson, Hammond, Anstie, and many others. It is true that the two last-named experimenters claim that *all* the alcohol taken is not again excreted without change, but that an adult individual is capable of retaining in some way a small quantity, averaging, according to Dr. Anstie, from four hundred to six hundred grains of alcohol in the twenty-four hours. This small quantity, equal only to about one ounce, was supposed by these gentlemen to be used up in the generation of some kind of *force*, but what kind of *force* remains a mystery. The truth is that the loss of such an amount of alcohol from a given quantity circulating with the blood during twenty-four hours is no more than might be held in mere mechanical union with the albuminous constituents of the tissues, for which it has a strong affinity; and the only *force* it develops is the catalytic *force* of *inertia*, by which it holds in check those natural molecular changes that would take place were it not present. Without further explanations, the effects of alcohol upon the human system may be clearly stated in the following brief paragraphs:

1. It is absorbed from the stomach and circulates with the blood, and is finally eliminated through the excretory organs as a foreign agent incapable of either digestion or assimilation.

2. While present in the blood it acts directly as an anæsthetic, diminishing the sensibility and force of both the cerebro-spinal and vaso-motor nervous centers; and as an organic sedative, diminishing molecular changes in the tissues and excretory organs, lessening the evolution of heat, and remotely favoring tissue degenerations and accumulations of waste material in the system.

This leads us to the third and last question proposed at the commencement of this paper—namely, What are the conditions in sickness that alcoholic liquors are calculated to remove?

In the foregoing brief review it has been shown that alcohol acts upon the human system as an anæsthetic, organic sedative, and antipyretic, and a skillful physician may use it in any case of disease where either or all these effects are needed, provided he can not have at hand any other agent or agents with which he can accomplish the same purposes more promptly and with less danger of any collateral injury to his patient. This proviso, however, if honestly attended to, will *practically exclude alcohol from the list of ordinary remedial agents.*

As an anæsthetic and anodyne, all will agree that it is

far inferior to and less manageable than ether, chloroform, nitrous oxide, and the ordinary narcotics.

As an organic sedative and antipyretic it is so much less prompt and efficient in its action than either water applied externally or the internal use of quinine, salicylic acid, digitalis, and a score of other articles, that no well-informed practitioner would think of selecting it for these purposes. Really, at the present time there are but two pretenses, or supposed morbid conditions, for which alcoholic remedies are prescribed by the enlightened part of the profession. One of these is that popularly prevalent condition of *exhaustion* or impairment from overwork, mental or physical, or from excessive drains by nursing or unnatural discharges.

It is in this large class of half-invalids that the moderate daily use of beer, ale, wine, and occasionally stronger alcoholic drinks is prescribed, on the plea that this power to retard the waste of tissues is conservative and equivalent to the addition of new matter by assimilation, the utter fallacy of which we have already indicated with sufficient clearness.

The other morbid condition for which these agents are very generally prescribed is that weakness of the heart sometimes met with in low forms of fever and in the advanced stage of other acute diseases.

It is claimed that alcohol is capable of strengthening and sustaining the action of the heart under the circumstances just named, and also under the first depressing influence of severe shock.

There is nothing in the ascertained physiological action of alcohol on the human system, as developed by a wide range of experimental investigation, to sustain this claim. Indeed it is difficult to conceive how it is possible that an agent which so plainly and directly diminishes nerve sensibility and voluntary muscular action can at the same time act as a cordial or heart-tonic. I have used the sphygmograph and every other available means for testing experimentally the effects of alcohol upon the action of the heart and blood-vessels generally, but have failed in every instance to get proof of any increased force of cardiac action.

The first and very transient effect is generally increased frequency of beat, followed immediately by dilatation of the peripheral vessels from impaired vaso-motor sensibility and the same unsteady or wavy sphygmographic tracing as is given in typhoid fever, and which is usually regarded as evidence of cardiac debility. Sometimes when the doses of alcohol are increased to the extent of decided anæsthesia the heart acts slower and the arteries have more volume from the increased obstruction to the movement of the blood through the capillaries and smaller vessels, and the diminished oxygenation and decarbonization of the blood in the lungs. Turning from the field of experimentation to the sick-room, my search for the power of alcohol to sustain the force of the heart or in any way to strengthen the patient has been equally unsuccessful. I was educated and entered upon the practice of medicine at a time when alcoholic drinks were universally regarded as stimulating and heat-producing in their influence on the human system, and commenced their use without prejudice or preconceived notions. But the first ten years of direct clinical or practical observation satisfied me fully of the incorrectness of those views, and very nearly banished the use of these agents from my list of remedies. And while it is true that during the last thirty years I have not prescribed for internal use the aggregate amount of one quart of any kind of fermented or distilled drinks, either in private or hospital practice, yet I have continued to have abundant opportunities for observing the effects of these agents as given by others with whom I have been in council; and simple truth compels me to say that I have never yet seen a case in which the use of alcoholic drinks either increased the force of the heart's action or strengthened the patient beyond the first thirty minutes after it was swallowed.

But I could detail very many cases in which the free administration of alcoholic remedies was quieting the patient's restlessness, enfeebling the capillary and peripheral circulation, and steadily favoring increased passive or hypostatic engorgements of the lungs and other internal viscera, and thereby hastening a fatal result, where both attending physicians and friends thought they were the only agents that were keeping the patient alive. Yet, persuading the abandonment of their use and the substitution of simple nourishment, aided by such nerve-excitants as tea, coffee, carbonate of ammonia, camphor, strychnia, etc., judiciously administered, instead of further prostration or sinking in consequence of such withdrawal, there has generally been a slow but steady improvement in all cases where improvement was possible, and in no case has it been found necessary or advisable to return to the use of alcoholic articles after they had been abandoned. If I am asked why, under such a statement of facts, the profession continues to prescribe these drinks, I answer, Simply from the force of habit and traditional education, coupled with a reluctance to risk the experiment of omitting them while the general popular notions sanction their use. Nothing is easier than self-deception in this matter. A patient is suddenly taken with syncope, or nervous weakness, from which abundant experience has shown that a speedy recovery would take place by simple rest and fresh air. But in the alarm of patients and friends something must be done. A little wine or brandy is given, and as it is not sufficient to positively prevent, the patient in due time revives, just as would have been the case if neither wine nor brandy had been used. Of course both doctor and friends will regard the so-called stimulant as the cause of the recovery. So, too, when patients are getting weak, in the advanced stage of fever or some other self-limited disease, an abundance of nourishment is regularly administered, in the greater part of which is mixed some kind of alcoholic drink. The latter will always occupy the chief attention, and if, after a severe run, the fever or disease finally disappears, it will be said that the patient was sustained or " kept alive " for over two or three weeks, as the case may be, " solely by the stimulants," when, in fact, if the same nourishment and care had been given without a drop of alcohol, he would have convalesced sooner and more perfectly, as I have seen demonstrated a thousand times during the last thirty years. Indeed, if any one will take the trouble to examine and analyze carefully the records of the large general hospitals, of both Europe and America, for the last half-century, I venture the statement that the ratio of mortality from general fevers and acute diseases will be found to have increased, *pari passu*, with the increase in the quantity of alcoholic drinks consumed in their treatment. A similar examination of the vital statistics of different nations and communities will show a close relation between the relative mortality from consumption, scrofula, apoplexy, paralysis, and hepatic, cardiac, and renal dropsies and the amount of alcoholic drinks consumed by the people.

By BENJAMIN WARD RICHARDSON, M. D., LL. D., AUTHOR OF "RESULTS OF RESEARCHES ON ALCOHOL."

I sought for certain knowledge. To the research I devoted three years, modifying experiments in every conceivable way, taking advantage of seasons and varying temperatures of season, extending observation from one class of animals to another, and making comparative researches with other bodies of the alcohol series than the ethylic or common alcohol.

The results I confess were as surprising to me as to any one else. They were surprising from their definiteness and their uniformity. * * * My experimental inquiries led me to discern, without original intention of discernment, that the power for which alcohol is esteemed, its power as an agent to liberate the heart, to excite the nervous centers and influence the passions, to afterwards congest the centers and dull the passions, to make men violent and mad, then imbecile and palsied. is, all through, one power in various stages of development and degree—a power not exercised for the elevation, but for the reduction of all the functions of life.   *   *   *   *   *

I learned purely by experimental observation that in its action on the living body this chemical substance, alcohol, deranges the constitution of the blood, unduly excites the heart and respiration, paralyzes the minute blood-vessels, increases and decreases according to the degree of its application the functions of the digestive organs, of the liver and of the kidneys, disturbs the regularity of nervous action, lowers the animal temperature, and lessens the muscular power.   *   *   *   *   *

It will be asked, Was there no evidence of any useful service rendered by the agent in the midst of so much obvious evidence of bad service? I answer to that question that there was no such evidence whatever, and there is none.

It has been urged that alcohol aids digestion, and so far is useful. I support, in reply, the statement of the late Dr. Cheyne, that nothing more effectually hinders digestion than alcohol.

I hold that those who abstain from alcohol have the best digestion, and that more instances of indigestion, of flatulency, of acidity, and of depression of mind and body are produced by alcohol than by any other single cause.   *   *
It is an agent as potent for evil as it is helpless for good.

OPINIONS BY OTHERS.

"I can see nothing in the action of alcohol in the human body, in any case or at any time, but that of a paralyzer; and I see in that view the key by which we can explain all the contradictory phenomena and all the contra-

14

dictory benefits which have been ascribed to the influence
of alcohol."—Dr. Edmunds, of London, in the *Lancet*.

"I thought I would do with as little as possible of alcoholic stimulants, and was thus led to try cautiously to do
without them in cases in which before they had been administered. The result of these trials was very decidedly
in favor of abstinence, and consequently alcoholic drinks
have legitimately disappeared from my list of medicines."
—Dr. Mudge.

"I have amply tried both ways. I gave alcohol in my
practice for twenty years, and have now practiced without
it for the last thirty years or more. My experience is that
acute disease is more readily cured without it, and chronic
disease much more manageable. I have not found a single
patient injured by the disuse of alcohol, or a constitution
requiring it."—Dr. Higginbottom.

Dr. Henderson, of Shanghai, and Dr. Bishop, of Naples,
reported the results of fever treatment without alcoholics
as reducing the mortality from twenty-eight to seven per
cent.; and Dr. Lees says that "every trial in the British
hospitals, in the treatment of particular diseases without
spirits, or with vastly reduced quantities of alcoholics, has
been, without exception, succeeded by a largely lessened
mortality."

Dr. Beaumont, lecturer on Materia Medica in Sheffield
Medical School, says: "I have treated several thousands
of cases of all kinds occurring in general practice without
alcoholic liquors of any kind, and have been gratified with
the successful results. The medicines take effect more po-
tently, and answer their end better."

Dr. John Blackmer says:

"Another consideration that should certainly have weight
with the physician in prescribing alcoholics is the extensive, yea, the almost universal adulteration of these articles.

"While it is, of course, conceded that the fact of adul-

15

terations is no argument against the use of the pure arti-
cle, yet if the adulteration is so flagrant and extensive that
it is altogether probable in any case, however extreme your
caution, that you have a base imitation and not the real
thing, the careful physician who cannot remedy this condition of things will seek some reliable substitute. It has
been asserted, and probably with truth, that ' not one per
cent. of all the liquor sold as brandy in this country is real
brandy.'

" Now, as no physician can tell, without a chemical anal-
ysis, what his patient is swallowing when he prescribes gin,
brandy, whiskey, or wine, we submit that he should either
strike alcoholics from his list of remedies, or he should
only employ pure alcohol.

"; Every one of these fluids is prescribed, if prescribed at
all, on account of the alcohol which it contains; and not
one of them would be employed as a beverage or a medicine if the alcohol were left out.

" Another consideration that should have weight with
the physician is the fascinating power of these fluids, and
the appetite for them which repeated doses are very certain to awaken.

" Such a risk should not be needlessly run.

" It should be remembered, too, that there are those who
are especially susceptible to the appetite for strong drink ;
a few doses arouse the passion. Indeed, everybody knows
that there are those who, on account of previous habits or
inherited tendencies, cannot safely even taste these articles. A single indulgence is like firing a magazine ; the
whole system is on fire in a moment, and they must and
will have more. No medical man has a right to awaken
such an appetite under any circumstances, even though in-
toxicants were invaluable as remedies, much less when our
medical armory is complete without them."